LANGLEY ADAMS LIBRARY

Missouri

By Christine Taylor-Butler

ER 917.78

Consultants
Reading Adviser
Nanci R. Vargus, EdD
Assistant Professor of Literacy
University of Indianapolis, Indianapolis, Indiana

Subject Adviser
Vicky Baker
Mid-Continent Public Library
Independence, Missouri

Children's Press®
A Division of Scholastic Inc.
New York   Toronto   London   Auckland   Sydney
Mexico City   New Delhi   Hong Kong
Danbury, Connecticut

$20.50

School.
6-08

Designer: Herman Adler Design
Photo Researcher: Caroline Anderson
The photo on the cover shows rhyolite formations at Johnson's Shut-Ins
State Park, Ozark Mountains, Missouri.

Library of Congress Cataloging-in-Publication Data

Taylor-Butler, Christine.
  Missouri / by Christine Taylor-Butler.
      p. cm. — (Rookie read-about geography)
  Includes index.
  ISBN 0-516-25258-5 (lib. bdg.)   0-516-25193-7 (pbk.)
  1. Missouri—Juvenile literature. 2. Missouri–Geography–Juvenile literature.
I. Title. II. Series.
  F466.3.T395 2005
  917.78'02–dc22   2004029766

CHILDREN'S PRESS, and ROOKIE READ-ABOUT®,
and associated logos are trademarks and/or registered trademarks
of Scholastic Library Publishing. SCHOLASTIC and associated logos
are trademarks and/or registered trademarks of Scholastic Inc.

1 2 3 4 5 6 7 8 9 10 R 14 13 12 11 10 09 08 07 06 05

Do you know why Missouri
is called the Show Me State?

People in Missouri like
to see things before they
believe them.

Missouri is in the middle
of the United States. It
touches eight other states.

Can you find Missouri on
this map?

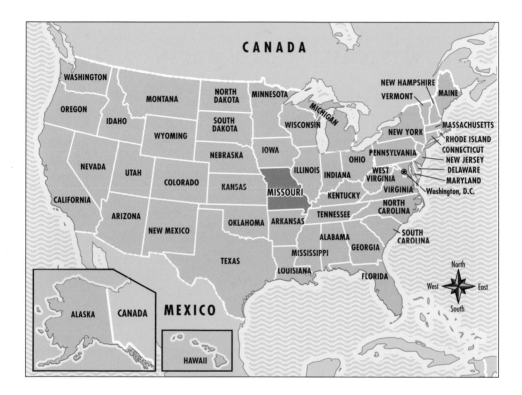

The state bird is the
bluebird. It lives in
Missouri from early
spring until November.

The state flower is the
white hawthorn blossom.

There are many rivers and streams in Missouri. People like to fish in them.

Bald eagles make their nests nearby.

The area in northern Missouri is called the Glaciated Till Plains. Long ago, large sheets of ice called glaciers crossed this land.

The soil in the Glaciated Till Plains is rich and black. It is perfect for farming.

Corn, wheat, and soybeans
are important crops here.

The Missouri River
flows from Kansas City
in the west to Saint Louis
in the east.

South of the Missouri River is the Ozark Highland. This part of Missouri has rocky soil, forests, mountains, and caves.

Taum Sauk is the highest mountain in Missouri.

More than 150 kinds of trees grow in Missouri.

The state tree is the flowering dogwood.

Missouri has more than 5,600 caves. No other state has more! These limestone caves are filled with stalagmites and stalactites.

stalagmites

stalactites

This is a salamander.

Bats, fish, and salamanders live in the caves.

The western part of
Missouri is called the
Osage Plains. Cows
and pigs are raised on
ranches here.

A machine dumps soybeans into a grain cart.

The southeastern tip of
Missouri is called the
Mississippi Lowlands.

The land was once a
swamp. Now farmers grow
cotton, soybeans, and rice
on the flat land.

Kansas City is the largest city in Missouri. It is famous for livestock and manufacturing.

Jefferson City is the state capital.

Saint Louis is another large city in Missouri.

The Gateway Arch is there. The arch is 630 feet tall. People can ride a tram to the top.

Maybe you will visit Missouri one day. You can explore caves. You can take a paddleboat ride, too.

What would you like to see in Missouri?

Words You Know

bald eagle

bluebird

cave

cows

dogwood trees

Gateway Arch

salamander

Taum Sauk Mountain

31

Index

About the Author

Christine Taylor-Butler is a freelance writer. She graduated from the Massachusetts Institute of Technology. She lives in Kansas City, Missouri.

Photo Credits

Photographs © 2005: AP/Wide World Photos: 11 (The St. Joseph News-Press, Ival Lawhon Jr.); Bruce Coleman Inc.: 26, 31 top left (Janis Burger), 6, 30 top right (Wayne Lankinen); Buddy Mays/Travel Stock: 3; Corbis Images: 15, 31 bottom right (David Muench), 21, 31 top right (Richard Hamilton Smith), 8 (Dale C. Spartas); Missouri Division of Tourism: 18, 30 bottom left; Photo Researchers, NY: 9, 30 top left (Tom & Pat Leeson), 19, 31 bottom left (Charles E. Mohr); Photri Inc./Darrell Mann: 22; The Image Works: 29 (David Frazier), 12 (Michael Siluk); Tom Till Photography, Inc.: cover, 16, 30 bottom right; Visuals Unlimited/Marty Delong: 7.
Maps by Bob Italiano